When you LIVE ALONE

Things Dedicated Singles Do

Cartoons by Benjamin

ELEVATION PRESS
OF COLORADO

When You Live Alone
Things Dedicated Singles Do

by D. P. Benjamin

Copyright © 2025 by Donald Paul Benjamin

For more information, please see *About the Author* at the close of this book and visit benjaminauthor.com

Cover design and interior design and formatting by Donna Marie Benjamin of Elevation Press of Colorado.

Elevation Press of Colorado
P.O. Box 603
Cedaredge, CO 81413

Ordering information: Quantity sales. Special discounts are available on quantity purchases by book clubs, corporations, associations, and others. For details, contact the publisher at the address above.

ISBN 978-0-932624-00-0

1. Main category — [Wit and humor] 2. Other category — [Comics]

ELEVATION PRESS
OF COLORADO

Cedaredge, Colorado
www.benjaminauthor.com

For information about other books by this author,
please see the final page of this book.

WHEN YOU LIVE ALONE

benjamin

there's nobody to pass
a cat's cradle to.

WHEN YOU LIVE ALONE

you can have the waterbed
to yourself.

WHEN YOU LIVE ALONE

benjamin

you can change the channel
whenever you want to.

WHEN YOU LIVE ALONE

you can shop without a cart.

WHEN YOU LIVE ALONE

every bill has your name on it.

WHEN YOU LIVE ALONE

you have to fill it up...

and, **you** have to zip it up.

WHEN YOU LIVE ALONE

benjamin

you entertain yourself.

WHEN YOU LIVE ALONE

you peek on crosswords.

benjamin

WHEN YOU LIVE ALONE

you can **fudge** on your diet.

WHEN YOU LIVE ALONE

laundry is a four-letter word!

WHEN YOU LIVE ALONE

benjamin

you have lots of hot water.

WHEN YOU LIVE ALONE

benjamin

you can rearrange a room.

WHEN YOU LIVE ALONE

you can experiment with a meal.

WHEN YOU LIVE ALONE

you can make your own music.

WHEN YOU LIVE ALONE

benjamin

you **always** get stuck
with the laundry.

WHEN YOU LIVE ALONE

you check the mailbox twice.

WHEN YOU LIVE ALONE

your buttons fall off.

WHEN YOU LIVE ALONE

you ask yourself three questions:

(1) Did the landline ring
while I was out?

(2) What's for supper?

(3) Who dirtied all these dishes?

WHEN YOU LIVE ALONE

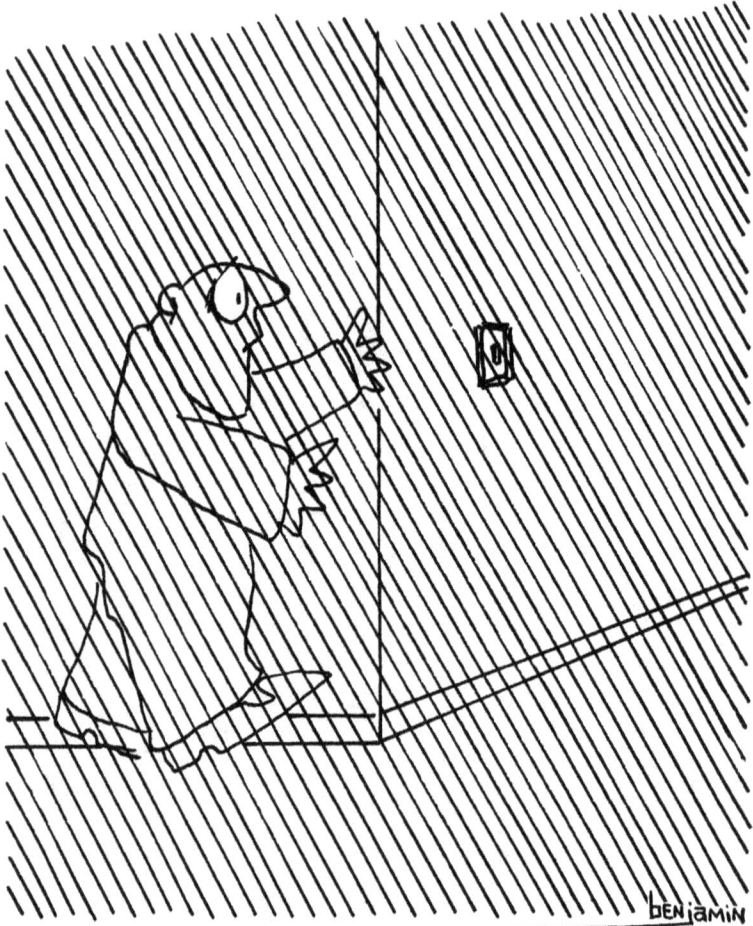

there's no one to turn
the light on for you...

in fact, there's no one
to turn on **period!**

WHEN YOU LIVE ALONE

you clean up when you
feel like it.

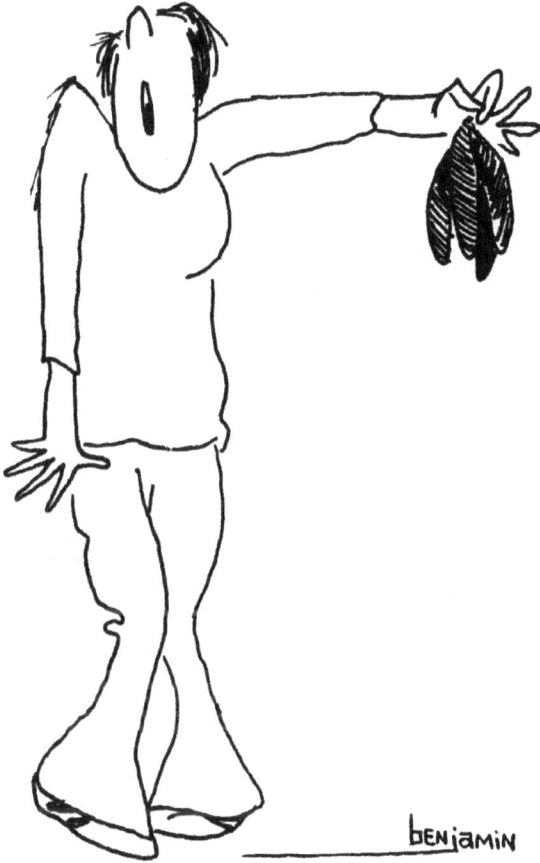

WHEN YOU LIVE ALONE

benjamin

your bananas turn brown.

WHEN YOU LIVE ALONE

you fix it yourself.

WHEN YOU LIVE ALONE

you have just enough dishes.

WHEN YOU LIVE ALONE

the doorbell always rings
at the wrong time.

WHEN YOU LIVE ALONE

you have too much bread.

WHEN YOU LIVE ALONE

you have too many
coat hangers.

WHEN YOU LIVE ALONE

you eat your own cooking.

WHEN YOU LIVE ALONE

you wash...

and, **you** dry.

WHEN YOU LIVE ALONE

benjamin

your bed-warmer
doesn't snore.

WHEN YOU LIVE ALONE

FRED

PISCES

PHIL

TOASTY

benjamin

everything has a name.

WHEN YOU LIVE ALONE

you make faces
in the mirror.

WHEN YOU LIVE ALONE

you oil your own back.

WHEN YOU LIVE ALONE

your chess set gets dusty.

WHEN YOU LIVE ALONE

it's **your** lawn.

WHEN YOU LIVE ALONE

and when you're locked out,
you're **really** locked out!

WHEN YOU LIVE ALONE

you have to tiptoe across the icy
floor in search of your slippers.

WHEN YOU LIVE ALONE

there's no one to tell
a nightmare to.

WHEN YOU LIVE ALONE

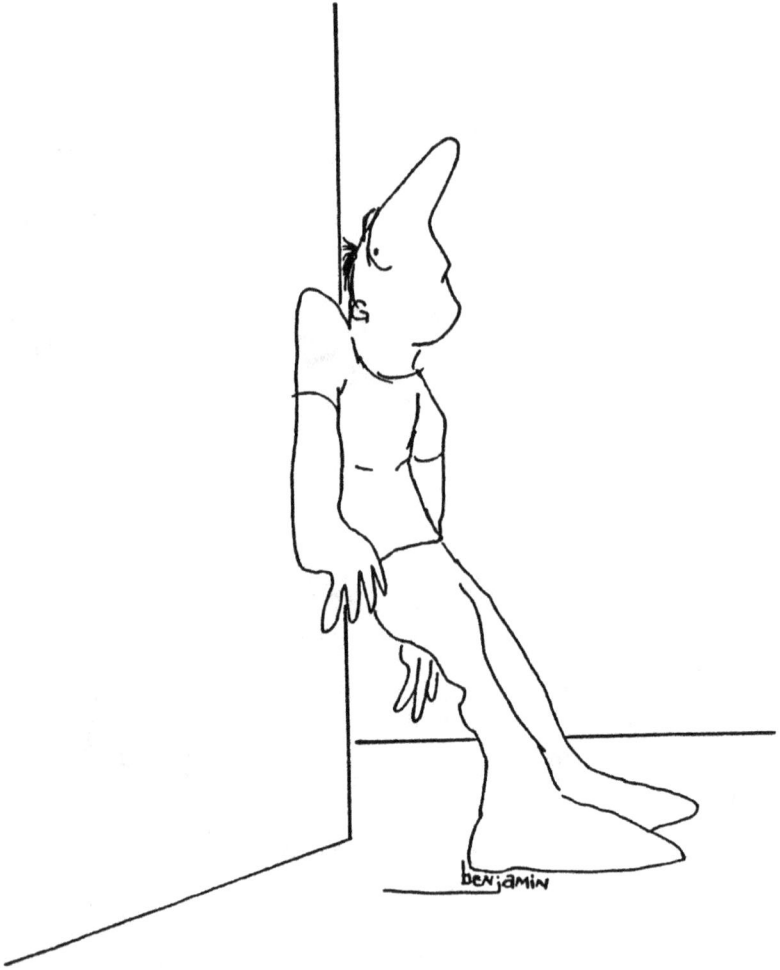

you rub your own back.

WHEN YOU LIVE ALONE

there's no one to blame
when you oversleep.

WHEN YOU LIVE ALONE

you can sing **outside**
the shower.

WHEN YOU LIVE ALONE

benjamin

you can use the same
bar of soap for five months.

WHEN YOU LIVE ALONE

you can find your toothbrush.

WHEN YOU LIVE ALONE

it's quiet when you go to bed.

WHEN YOU LIVE ALONE

benjamin

you don't have to wait
for the funnies.

WHEN YOU LIVE ALONE

you talk to yourself...
a lot!

WHEN YOU LIVE ALONE

benjamin

your pets don't experience
divided loyalties.

WHEN YOU LIVE ALONE

you lose your key.

WHEN YOU LIVE ALONE

you eat a lot of tuna fish.

WHEN YOU LIVE ALONE

it's **your** litter box to clean.

WHEN YOU LIVE ALONE

you can sleep in.

WHEN YOU LIVE ALONE

you can coax a garden.

WHEN YOU LIVE ALONE

you have too much spaghetti.

WHEN YOU LIVE ALONE

you must have patience.

WHEN YOU LIVE ALONE

you always know
what's in your lunchbox.

WHEN YOU LIVE ALONE

benjamin

you service your own car.

WHEN YOU LIVE ALONE

benjamin

you wax your own skiis.

WHEN YOU LIVE ALONE

benjamin

you can really get into a book.

WHEN YOU LIVE ALONE

you know who your friends are.

WHEN YOU LIVE ALONE

you take care of yourself!

ABOUT THE AUTHOR

Donald Paul Benjamin is a Colorado native, an award winning novelist, free-lance cartoonist, and journalist. He also writes about Western Colorado history. He is the author of *The Four Corners Mystery Series, The Great Land Fantasy Series, The Surface Creek Life Series,* a *Cartoon Series,* and a *Children's Series.*

Photo by Rève Studios
Cedaredge, Colorado

In addition to his writing career, he also works as a freelance journalist, cartoonist, and photographer. A U.S. Army veteran, he served three years as a military journalist and illustrator, including a tour in Korea. Trained as a teacher of reading, he has worked with a wide variety of learners from those attending kindergarten to college students. He also holds an advanced degree in college administration. He lived in Arizona and worked in higher education for more than three decades before retiring in 2014.

He now lives in Cedaredge, a small town on the Western Slope of Colorado, where he hikes and fishes in the surrounding wilderness. He and his wife, Donna Marie, operate Elevation Press of Colorado.

Email: elevationpressbooks@gmail.com
Studio Phone: 970-856-9891
Mail: D.P. Benjamin, P.O. Box 603, Cedaredge, CO 81413
Website: https://benjaminauthor.com/
Visit the Author's Facebook Page under: D.P. Benjamin Author
Instagram: https://www.instagram.com/benjaminnovelist/

The Four Corners Mystery Series
- Book 1: *The Road to Lavender*
- Book 2: *A Lavender Wedding*
- Book 3: *Spirits of Grand Lake*
- Book 4: *The War Nickel Murders*
- Book 5: *Rare Earth*
- Book 6: *Walking Horse Ranch*
- Book 7: *Lavender Farewell*

Cartoon Series
- *When You Live Alone*
- *Downhill*
- *Further Downhill*
- *Ski Zoo*

Children's Series
- *Hibiscus the Lion*

The Great Land Fantasy Series
- Book 1: *Stone Bride*

The Surface Creek Life Series
- Book 1: *A Surface Creek Christmas: Winter Tales 1904–1910*

Mountain: A Cautionary Tale
- Book 1 and Book 2

In paperback or Kindle on **amazon.com** and **barnesandnoble.com**.